Too much CARBON

T0011151

Carbon

This is **coal.**

Carbon is in the coal.

This is **oil.**

Carbon is in the oil.

The coal and the oil will burn and make a gas.

The gas is here ...

and here ...

and here.

Plants need carbon

Look at the trees.

The trees need

the carbon to grow.

The grass needs

the carbon to grow too.

Too much carbon

There is too much carbon.

There is too much carbon here ...

and here ...

and here.

Too much carbon is not good for us.

It is not good for our **world.**

Helping our world

Look at us.

We are helping our world.

We are planting trees.

14

The carbon will stay in the trees.

Glossary

 coal

 oil

 world